Dwight Howard
A Basketball Star Who Cares

John Albert Torres

Enslow Elementary

an imprint of

Enslow Publishers, Inc.
40 Industrial Road
Box 398
Berkeley Heights, NJ 07922
USA

http://www.enslow.com

Enslow Elementary, an imprint of Enslow Publishers, Inc.

Enslow Elementary® is a registered trademark of Enslow Publishers, Inc.

Library of Congress Cataloging-in-Publication Data

Torres, John Albert
  Dwight Howard : a basketball star who cares / John A. Torres.
    p. cm. — (Sports stars who care)
  Includes bibliographical references and index.
  Summary: "This sports biography tells the story of basketball all-star Dwight Howard, and how with the help of his family, he has become one of the most feared big men in the game. But even off of the court, Dwight has shown he is a sports star who cares"—Provided by publisher.
  ISBN 978-0-7660-4294-0
  1. Howard, Dwight—Juvenile literature. 2. Basketball players—United States—Biography—Juvenile literature. I. Title.
  GV884.H68T67 2013
  796.323092—dc23
  [B]
                            2012039420

Paperback ISBN: 978-1-4644-0533-4
EPUB ISBN: 978-1-4645-1272-8
Single-User PDF ISBN: 978-1-4646-1272-5
Multi-User PDF ISBN: 978-0-7660-5904-7

052013 Lake Book Manufacturing, Inc., Melrose Park, IL

Printed in the United States of America

10 9 8 7 6 5 4 3 2 1

To Our Readers:
We have done our best to make sure all Internet addresses in this book were active and appropriate when we went to press. However, the author and the Publisher have no control over, and assume no liability for, the material available on those Internet sites or on other Web sites they may link to. Any comments or suggestions can be sent by e-mail to comments@enslow.com or to the address on the back cover.

♻ Enslow Publishers, Inc., is committed to printing our books on recycled paper. The paper in every book contains 10% to 30% post-consumer waste (PCW). The cover board on the outside of each book contains 100% PCW. Our goal is to do our part to help young people and the environment too!

Photo Credits: AP Images/Alex Menendez, p. 42; AP Images/Dusan Vranic/Pool, p. 9; AP Images/Ed Betz, pp. 15, 24; AP Images/Eric Gay, pp. 11, 12, 30; AP Images/John Amis, p. 17; AP Images/John Raoux, pp. 26, 35, 41; AP Images/Linda Spillers/Nike, p. 23; AP Images/Lu Tong/Color China Photo, p. 4; AP Images/Mark J. Terrill, p. 1; AP Images/Phelan M. Ebenhack, pp. 20, 33, 39; AP Images/PRNewsFoto/D12 Foundation, p. 7; AP Images/Reed Saxon, p. 36; AP Images/Yun Long/Imaginechina, p. 28.

Cover Photo: AP Images/Mark J. Terrill

Contents

Dwight Howard has actually been told that he smiles too much.

What his critics do not realize is that even though he is happy and smiling all the time, inside there is a fierce competitor. He wants nothing more than to win basketball games and help bring his team a championship.

The truth is that Dwight Howard is probably the best defensive player in all of basketball!

Just ask any NBA player who has dribbled into the lane going for a layup or a slam dunk only to have No. 12, Superman, Dwight Howard come flying out of nowhere to block the shot. They will tell you that Howard can fool you with his smiling face and happy-go-lucky attitude.

Even though he is still a young player, Howard has led the NBA in rebounding four times. He's led the league in blocked shots twice, and he became the first player in history to be named the

NBA Defensive Player of the Year three seasons in a row. He has even won a gold medal playing basketball for the United States in the Summer Olympics.

But Howard is much more than what you see on the basketball court. And that is likely the reason for the smile. He is a man of faith who loves helping others just as much, if not more, than jumping high in the air to grab a rebound or send someone's shot sailing out of bounds.

He has become involved with several charitable organizations. This includes the D12 Foundation that he started to help young people in poverty-stricken areas. But that is not all. He has sponsored a room at the Florida Hospital for Children. He has opened a learning center in Orlando, and served as a goodwill ambassador on trips around the world. He has even gotten involved with the Boys & Girls Clubs of Central Florida.

Now that Dwight is a member of the Los Angeles Lakers, his foundation and charitable reach will extend all the way to the West Coast.

Howard plays video games with two young people in the Dwight Howard Teen Room at the Florida Hospital for Children. The room was built with funds from his D12 Foundation.

Alex Martins helped run Howard's old team—the Orlando Magic—for many years. He praised Howard for his good deeds.

"There are other players who have done a significant amount for the community," Martins said. "But I've been here now seventeen of the team's twenty-two years, and in that time, there hasn't been a player who has done more than Dwight has."

7

wight Howard was already one of the most respected and feared NBA superstars when he was asked to be part of the U.S. Men's Basketball Team. It would be competing during the Summer Olympics in China in 2008.

Howard had already been an NBA All-Star and led the league

Chapter 1

Going for Gold

Leaping high above the rim, Dwight Howard throws down a dunk in the 2008 Summer Olympics. In this game, the United States beat Spain, 119–82.

in several categories when he was picked. But suddenly the star center for the Orlando Magic was feeling a little worried, a little nervous. He realized that there was nothing he wanted more than to win the gold medal for his country.

A day before flying to China with his teammates, he was all alone sprinting on the track at Jones High School in Orlando. But when he raised his head he noticed a group of people had gathered to watch him. They started yelling encouragement, "Come on Dwight! You have to do this for America!" Then they started chanting "U-S-A, U-S-A!"

Dwight was humbled and honored to be part of the team. The team boasted such NBA stars as Kobe Bryant, Jason Kidd, Carmelo Anthony, and LeBron James, among others. But Howard's intense style of play and coolness under pressure was just what was needed.

During a very close game against Argentina, which had several NBA players on it, the U.S. team was in danger of being eliminated. It was early in the third quarter and the United States' lead had gone from 18

Dwight Howard leaps to defend Luis Scola of Argentina during the 2008 Olympics.

points to only six. It was as if the wind had been taken from the American team and the momentum was swinging the other way.

Howard was not asked to score much on a team with so many great offensive players. But he suddenly found himself free in the lane. He made eye contact with American point guard Jason Kidd, and before he knew it, the ball was in Dwight Howard's hands.

Howard rattled the rim with a tremendous slam dunk. A few seconds later the two players combined again, this time on a pick-and-roll. Again, Kidd found

11

Dwight Howard stands with some of his fellow Olympic stars as they receive their gold medals. From left to right are Chris Bosh, Dwight Howard, LeBron James, Carlos Boozer, and Michael Redd.

Howard with the ball. The big man threw it down to help the Americans open up a big lead.

Argentina knew there was no way they could stop the Americans, especially if Howard was going to get the ball down low so close to the basket. With about seven minutes left in the third quarter, and the game slipping away from Argentina, they tried to get Howard rattled and upset.

One of their players, Carlos Delfino, hit Howard very hard for an intentional foul. Players from both teams rushed at each other for a moment. But Howard kept his cool and flashed that big famous smile of his. Both teams backed off and continued playing basketball.

The United States went on to defeat Spain in the gold-medal game. Howard and his teammates stood proudly with the medals around their necks as they played the national anthem.

After it was over, Howard could breathe a sigh of relief. But he also knew that the team played its hardest in order to win the gold.

"We all were so proud to be representing our country," he said. "There was just no way that we were going to leave China without that gold medal."

A lot of people like to claim that basketball or some other sport is in their blood. But in Dwight Howard's case it actually might be true.

Howard's mother Sheryl loved playing basketball. In fact, in 1974 she was a player on the first

Chapter 2

Born to Play Basketball

Sheryl Howard, Dwight's mom, celebrates as her "miracle child" gets drafted first overall in the 2004 NBA Draft.

women's basketball team ever at Morris Brown College in Georgia. That is the state where Howard would later be born.

She even continues to play basketball today, often appearing in charity games with other mothers of famous athletes.

Sheryl always wanted a big family. But she had a hard time having a child after her two daughters were born. She lost seven children before birth and never thought she would be able to raise another child. When Dwight was born she cherished him and called him her "miracle child."

Dwight's father, Dwight Sr., was a Georgia State Trooper. He taught Dwight from a young age how important it was to live a clean life and to stay out of trouble with the law. He also loved basketball and coached at a small Christian school in Atlanta.

So when Dwight was born on December 8, 1985, it was very natural that there were balls almost everywhere he looked—even in his crib! When he was old enough to walk, Howard started playing basketball on a Nerf basketball hoop in his bedroom. Even back then, at a very young age, Howard enjoyed dunking the ball through the hoop.

With the help of his parents, who both loved sports, Howard learned how to dribble a basketball in his backyard when he was only three years old. The family lived in a town called Swainsboro. The three

Dwight Howard, Sr. (left), sits with Dwight. This was the news conference at which he announced he was entering the 2004 NBA Draft.

most important things in the household were church, school, and basketball.

The family was very religious and spent every Sunday at church. They were also very strict with Dwight. His mother worked at the courthouse before

17

becoming a teacher at Howard's school. She expected him to have his uniform pressed every night before going to bed and ready for the following day.

His parents were very involved in his day-to-day activities. They knew where he was at all times and the friends he was spending time with. Sometimes that would get Howard angry. But now, looking back, he realizes it was because they loved him so much.

"Trust me when I say this: Having parents who care about you and stay involved in your day-to-day activities is a very good thing," he said.

Howard liked to play a lot of sports while he was growing up. Most of the kids who lived in his rough neighborhood played basketball. There was a lot of crime and a lot of violence in the town where Howard grew up. But no one ever bothered him. That was probably because his dad was allowed to park his police

Chapter 3

Dreaming Big

One of the reasons Dwight Howard knew he would play in the NBA one day was because he was doing things like this in middle school.

car in the driveway of their home. Everyone knew that his dad was a law enforcement officer.

While Howard enjoyed playing many different sports, it was not until the age of nine that he made a discovery that would shape his future. He liked other sports just fine, but he found that he loved basketball. He started to get serious about it, playing every day after school and working on his skills to get better.

As he got older, Howard started having big dreams of one day playing in the NBA. He says it is important to have big dreams and to set your sights way up high. But it was not until a day in the eighth grade that Howard actually started believing in those dreams. He had just learned how to dunk a basketball and had become very confident on the court. He did not believe there was anyone who could stop him from scoring.

He was playing basketball on a court outside his school against a pair of older, bigger, and better players. At first, they did not even want him to play because they thought he was too small, too skinny, and too weak.

But play after play, Howard scored on them. Someone watching the game yelled out that Howard could make it to the NBA without ever going to college. He already had a list of his dreams and goals written down in his bedroom. Now he added another: He wanted to be the number one pick in the 2004 NBA Draft.

Now this was really a big dream. Almost everyone drafted into the NBA has played some college basketball. Here was a kid who was only in the eighth grade making this bold prediction.

But Howard kept growing while attending Atlanta Christian Academy High School. He soon developed into a great power forward. He worked very hard on his game but also his strength, speed, and endurance. He averaged more than 16 points per game in high school but saved the best for last. His senior year, Howard scored 25 points and 18 rebounds per game as he led his school to the state championship. He won all types of awards that season including being named the Gatorade Player of the Year and the McDonald's Player of the Year.

Howard clutches the MVP trophy from the 2004 Michael Jordan Capital Classic. It was one of many honors Howard received as a high school senior.

NBA Commissioner David Stern introduces Dwight as the No. 1 pick in the 2004 NBA Draft.

After talking it over with his parents, Howard decided to skip college and try and go into the NBA draft right out of high school. All that hard work proved to Howard that dreams, even really big ones, can come true. On June 24, 2004 the Orlando Magic selected Dwight Howard with the very first pick of the NBA draft.

Dwight Howard was going to the NBA!

Dwight Howard had his work cut out for him. The Magic once boasted such great players as Shaquille O'Neal and Penny Hardaway. Now the franchise had fallen on bad times. The team won only 21 games the season before Howard arrived.

Chapter 4

"It's a Bird, It's a Plane, It's Superman"

Dwight Howard looks to block a shot by Josh Smith of the Atlanta Hawks.

It was going to take a lot of work to get the squad back to prominence. The fans in Central Florida were frustrated. They were tired of seeing their team at the bottom of the standings. At first, some fans were unhappy with the pick.

Some people thought they should have selected more established college players like Emeka Okafor or Ben Gordon. Those players were chosen right after Howard. But Howard's play on the court soon won him many supporters.

He became the first rookie to come straight from high school and start every one of his team's 82 games. He also showed that he could be a low-post presence for years to come. He became the youngest player to average ten rebounds a game. One game, he even pulled down a whopping 20 boards!

But he still needed to get stronger. Sometimes he was pushed around on the court, and his offense was unpolished. After the season, Howard made the decision that he would always be the hardest working player on his team.

"I put in a lot of work to get to the NBA," he wrote on his own Web site. "So I figure if I do everything I need to do every day in the weight room and during practice I should be a dominant player."

He returned for his second season twenty pounds heavier and much stronger. He continued lifting weights and eating steak and potatoes whenever he

After his rookie season, Howard worked hard to become stronger. He is now one of the biggest and most muscular players in the league.

could. Soon his body started changing and he became very muscular.

Howard always loved Superman as a kid. He started modeling his body after the comic book hero. It was not long before he started playing like a super-man on the court. In a game against Charlotte, Howard became the youngest player to score 20 points and grab 20 rebounds in the same game. He finished second in the league in rebounding average and the team was slowly getting better, winning 36 games.

By his fourth season, Howard had established himself as an NBA superstar. His scoring average had increased every year in the league and it was now hovering about 20 points per game.

Dwight entered the Slam Dunk Contest held during the 2008 All-Star weekend. That was when the world really took notice of Dwight Howard in a big way. That was the weekend that one of the promising young players in the game became officially known as "Superman."

During the Slam Dunk Contest, Howard wore a blue Superman T-shirt that showed off his muscles.

Dressed as Superman, Howard wins the 2008 Slam Dunk Contest. His nickname has been Superman ever since.

Then he put on a red cape. The idea was to "fly" toward the basket and dunk the ball.

Howard took off around the foul line and started soaring. His leaping ability was always terrific, but this time he somehow got even higher. He caught a pass and held it high over his head with his right hand as he continued soaring toward the basket. Then in one fell swoop he threw down a ferocious dunk.

The crowd erupted with cheers. He scored a perfect "10" and Dwight Howard, the kid who dreamed of playing in the NBA, was now officially a superhero. In Orlando, he was becoming a legend. Howard led the team to the playoffs that season for the first time in years.

"Having the chance to impersonate Superman had been a dream of mine since I was a kid," Howard said. "I always thought he was the coolest dude on the planet."

By 2009, Dwight Howard had just about single-handedly transformed the Orlando Magic into a championship caliber team. He led the team to its second straight playoff berth and the top seed in the Eastern Conference.

The Magic squeaked by the Philadelphia 76ers in the first round

CHAPTER 5

Coast to Coast

Dwight Howard and LeBron James fight for a loose ball during the 2009 Eastern Conference Finals.

of the playoffs. Next, they defeated a very tough Boston Celtics team. Then they faced LeBron James and the Cleveland Cavaliers in the Eastern Conference Finals. With the Magic leading the series three games to two, Howard played the best game of his career. His effort would send the Magic to the NBA Finals against the Los Angeles Lakers.

During that Game 6 against Cleveland, Howard put his team on his shoulders and carried them. He scored 40 points and had 14 rebounds. Now the Magic were going to the NBA Finals for the first time in fourteen years.

But the Lakers, led by Kobe Bryant, were too much for the Magic. Los Angeles won the series and the NBA championship in five games. Unfortunately, that was the closest Howard came to bringing a championship to Central Florida.

The next few seasons for the Magic were similar. The team had a roster filled with average players and one great one, Howard. They would always win a lot of regular season games but fail in the playoffs.

Howard started getting frustrated and thought it might be time to move on. The Magic were clearly starting to enter a rebuilding phase. He wanted to be traded to a team that had a chance to win the championship. It was a tough decision. The Orlando Magic fans pleaded with Howard to change his mind

Dwight Howard (left) and teammate Jameer Nelson (right) are bummed after their loss to the Lakers in the 2009 NBA Finals.

during a tough 2011–12 season. That year ended with Howard having to undergo back surgery and miss the playoffs.

Finally, after a lot of rumors, the Magic granted Howard his wish. He was traded across the country to the very team that once faced the Magic in the finals: the Los Angeles Lakers.

Howard was traded to
the Los Angeles Lakers
in August 2012.

Even though he always loved being "Superman," Howard would no longer have to act like a superhero. He was joining a team in Los Angeles that already had three superstar players on it: Kobe Bryant, Steve Nash, and Pau Gasol.

The Lakers always seemed to be in the hunt for the NBA title. Howard said he would miss the fans in Orlando, but was very excited to get started with his new team.

"I would like to thank the city of Orlando," Howard said as he was introduced to the media at a press conference in Los Angeles. "I wish the organization a lot of success. Now I'm happy to be a Laker. I'm so excited; it's really hard to talk. I couldn't sleep last night. It's time for a change for me and it's time for a change in Orlando."

Lakers fans hope that Howard will continue his superstar play for years to come. They will get a chance to see in person what Florida fans saw for years: that Dwight Howard plays the game with passion and intensity that is hard to match.

The truth about Dwight Howard is that he might save his best work and greatest deeds for the moments he is away from the basketball court and out of the spotlight.

Howard, like other athletes such as Tim Tebow and Jeremy Lin, has always been very open about his Christian faith. It is those

Chapter 6

Helping Others

One of Dwight's fans hugs him while talking strategy with him prior to a D12 charity bowling event.

religious beliefs, he says, that prompt him to do so much charitable work.

In fact, the moment Howard signed his first contract with the Magic, he established the Dwight D. and Sheryl H. Howard Foundation. It provides scholarships for underprivileged children to attend private schools. The charity has already given many children opportunities they would never have had without Howard's help.

But he does so much more.

Howard often visits sick children in hospitals in many of the cities he travels to with his basketball team. He also is one of the key people in the NBA's "Read to Achieve" program that encourages kids to read more.

Obviously, children are very important to him. Howard was recently named a special ambassador to the organization Big Brothers, Big Sisters that pairs children with adult mentors.

The superstar wants to help not only people in this country, but across the globe. In 2010 he started the Dwight Howard Fund to help at-risk children all over

Howard jokes around with former teammate Matt Barnes during a charity basketball event.

As part of the Dwight Howard Fund, he went to Haiti to talk with locals and play basketball with the children. The fund provided relief to families in need.

the world. He immediately started helping children in the poor Caribbean country of Haiti who had suffered through a horrific earthquake earlier that year.

It's amazing that he finds the time to do all this and at the same time help the NBA with its goal of spreading the game of basketball all over the world. He has taken trips to China, Taiwan, Africa, and India for the NBA during the offseason.

If there is a cause to help children, don't be surprised to see that Dwight Howard is somehow involved. He truly loves helping others, and that's one of the main reasons he seems to always be smiling.

"By smiling I can make other people smile too," he said. "And I love making people smile."

That is something Dwight Howard has mastered, on and off the court.

Career Statistics

Year	Team	G	FG	FG%	REB	AST	STL	BLK	PTS	PPG
2004–05	Orlando	82	352	.520	823	75	77	136	981	12.0
2005–06	Orlando	82	468	.531	1,022	125	65	115	1,292	15.8
2006–07	Orlando	82	526	.603	1,008	158	70	156	1,443	17.6
2007–08	Orlando	82	583	.599	1,161	110	74	176	1,695	20.7
2008–09	Orlando	79	560	.572	1,093	112	77	231	1,624	20.6
2009–10	Orlando	82	510	.612	1,082	144	75	228	1,503	18.3
2010–11	Orlando	78	619	.593	1,098	107	107	186	1,784	22.9
2011–12	Orlando	54	416	.573	785	104	81	116	1,113	20.6
2012–13	Lakers	76	470	.578	945	108	84	186	1,296	17.1
	TOTALS	697	4,504	.577	9,017	1,043	710	1,530	12,731	18.3

G = Games   REB = Rebounds   BLK = Blocks
FG = Field Goals   AST = Assists   PTS = Points
FG% = Field Goal Percentage   STL = Steals   PPG = Points Per Game

Where to Write

DWIGHT HOWARD
c/o LOS ANGELES LAKERS
555 N. Nash Street
El Segundo, CA 90245

ambassador—A representative who travels to promote a group.

Big Brothers, Big Sisters—A nonprofit group that pairs a young person with an adult mentor.

block—When a defensive player swats away a shot before it can reach the rim or backboard.

boards—In basketball, another name for rebounds.

charity—The giving of one's time or money to aid those less fortunate.

children's hospital—A medical center that focuses on treating young people.

Christian—One who follows the teachings of Jesus Christ, and believes he is the son of God.

courthouse—A place where legal business is conducted and trials are held.

defense—In basketball, the team without the ball that is attempting to stop the other team from scoring.

D12 Foundation—Nonprofit group started by Dwight Howard to aid children in unwealthy areas.

Dwight D. and Sheryl H. Howard Foundation—Foundation started by Dwight Howard to help benefit at-risk youth and families.

Dwight Howard Fund—A fund started by Dwight Howard and Adonal Foyle to support at-risk children around the world. The first check the fund wrote was to benefit earthquake survivors in Haiti.

Eastern Conference—One of the two conferences that make up the NBA. The other is the Western Conference.

foul—An illegal play in basketball.

layup—A basketball shot where a player scores by bouncing the ball off the backboard and into the hoop.

NBA—Short for the National Basketball Association, the premier basketball league in the world.

Olympics—An international athletic competition held every four years. Basketball is part of the Summer Olympics.

pick-and-roll—A basketball play in which an offensive player sets a screen for his teammate and then turns and heads toward the basket to receive the ball.

playoffs—A tournament held after the end of the regular season to determine the league champion.

poverty—A condition in which a person lives without much wealth or opportunity.

power forward—Position on the basketball court that plays close to the basket and is responsible mainly for rebounding.

Read to Achieve—A campaign started by the NBA that encourages adults to read with children.

rebound—The act of recovering the ball after a missed shot.

rebuilding phase—When a team begins to rid itself of established players in order to bring in younger players with more potential for the future.

slam dunk—A basketball shot where a player scores by pushing the ball through the rim.

sprint—A drill in which a person runs as fast as possible over a set distance.

weight room—A facility used for lifting weights and exercising.

Read More

Books

Basen, Ryan. *Dwight Howard: Gifted and Giving Basketball Star*. Berkeley Heights, N.J.: Enslow Publishers, Inc., 2012.

Howard, Dwight, and John Denton. *All You Can Be: Learning & Growing Through Sports*. Chicago, Ill.: Triumph Books, 2011.

Mattern, Joanne. *Dwight Howard: Basketball Superstar*. Mankato, Minn.: Capstone Press, 2011.

Internet Addresses

Dwight Howard Statistics
http://www.basketball-reference.com/players/h/howardw01.html

Official Website of the Los Angeles Lakes
http://www.nba.com/lakers/

Official Twitter Page:
http://twitter.com/DwightHoward

Index